This book belongs to:

....

EXPLORE AND INVENT

How this collection works

This book includes five fascinating non-fiction texts to encourage your child to explore their world in all its variety – and even zoom off into space! These lively texts are full of amazing facts and intriguing ideas, with the same high-quality artwork and photos you would expect from any non-fiction book – but they are specially written so that your child can read them for themselves. They are carefully levelled and in line with your child's phonics learning at school.

It's very important for your child to have access to non-fiction as well as stories, while they are learning to read. This helps them develop a wider range of reading skills, and prepares them for learning through reading. Most children love finding out about the world as they read – and some children prefer non-fiction to story books, so it's doubly important to make sure that they have opportunities to read both.

How to use this book

You can share this book with your child, encouraging them to read aloud to you, or your child can read it independently. Keep reading sessions fun by picking a time when your child is not distracted by other things, and when they are happy to concentrate for about 20 minutes. Encourage them to choose the non-fiction text they want to read, and talk to them about it afterwards. Read the tips on the next page, as they offer ideas and suggestions for getting the most out of this collection.

Tips for reading non-fiction

STEP 1

Before your child begins reading one of the non-fiction texts, look together at the contents page for that particular text. What does your child think the text will be about? Do they know anything about this subject already? Briefly talk about your child's ideas, and remind them of anything they know about the topic if necessary. Look at the page of notes and 'before reading' suggestions for each text, and use them to help introduce the text to your child.

STEP 2

Ask your child to show you some of the non-fiction features in the text – for example, the contents page, glossary and index, photos, labels and fact boxes. Can your child show you how to use the contents page and index? Flip through the text to get a sense of what it is about.

STEP 3

Ask your child to read the text aloud or silently. Encourage them to stop and look at the pictures, and talk about what they are reading. Your child will be able to read most of the words in the text, but if they struggle with a word, remind them to say the sounds in the word from left to right and then blend the sounds together to read the whole word, e.g. *a-t-m-o-s-ph-ere, atmosphere*. If they have real difficulty, tell them the word and move on.

STEP 4

When your child has finished reading, talk about what they have found out. Which bits of the text did they like most, and why? Encourage your child to do some of the fun activities that follow each text.

CONTENTS

OXFORD
UNIVERSITY PRESS

Way-out Day Out

An alien takes a child from Earth on a tour of the solar system and describes the sun and the incredible planets.

Before reading

Look at the contents list and read the planet names. Does your child know anything about these planets already?

Look out for ...

… a planet that gets really hot and really cold.

… a planet that could squash you like a tomato!

… a planet that has two moons shaped like potatoes.

… planets that have no solid ground.

… a dwarf planet.

WAY-OUT DAY OUT

CONTENTS

Rob Alcraft

The Sun

This is a perfect and **way-out** place to begin. The sun is the middle of your **solar system**. Everything else whizzes around it. It's a super-big, super-bright, burning ball of **gas**.

It's super-hot, too. If you get too close – *puff*! You'll burn up in a flash.

Massive, isn't it?

The sun is a **star**. The stars you see at night are like our sun, but much further away.

| the sun | 5700°C |

 pizza oven 200°C

Mercury

On Mercury you'll fry or you'll freeze!
It's really quite extreme.

Days are hotter than an **earthling** oven. Nights
are four times colder than your North Pole.

There's plenty of time to enjoy a day on
Mercury – every day is 59 Earth-days long!

Mercury is a rocky ball, about the size of Earth's **moon**.

Mercury today	430°C
boiling kettle	100°C
North Pole	– 40°C
Mercury tonight	– 180°C

Venus

This is what you call exciting!

If you went down there, you would get squashed like a tomato because the **atmosphere** is so heavy. Then you would get roasted! The thick clouds of gas trap a lot of heat.

Out you get!

What?!

Only kidding, earthling.

This is the surface of Venus.

Venus	462°C
pizza oven	200°C
boiling kettle	100°C

Mars

You'll like Mars – it's pretty. It has red rocks, a pink sky, and pink and blue clouds. There's loads to see, like the biggest volcano in your solar system. There's frozen water, dried-out rivers, exciting dust storms...

dust storm

Hang on, wasn't that Earth we just passed?

Don't worry, earthling – we're going back later.

big volcano

Mars is cold and rocky.

melting ice	0°C
Mars today	- 5°C
Mars tonight	- 87°C

Jupiter

Guess what, earthling? This planet has no ground!

Jupiter is mostly gas, not rock. A giant ball of gas! It's all cloudy and gassy on the outside. Inside, the gas gets squashed and that makes it soupy and thick.

It's like a gooey sweet with moons whizzing around it!

Wow! All that is gas?

This is Io (*say* igh-oa), one of Jupiter's 67 moons. It's covered in erupting volcanoes.

melting ice	0°C
North Pole	- 40°C
Jupiter	- 148°C

Jupiter's Great Red Spot is a giant storm.

17

Saturn

Don't you just love these rings?
They're made of lumps of rock and ice
circling around. Dreamy, aren't they?

Saturn has more than 60 moons, too.

rings

Is there any ground?

No. Saturn is another giant ball of gas.

This is the moon, Enceladus (*say* en-sel-a-dus). It has a fizzy ocean bubbling away inside it.

melting ice	0°C
North Pole	– 40°C
Saturn	– 178°C

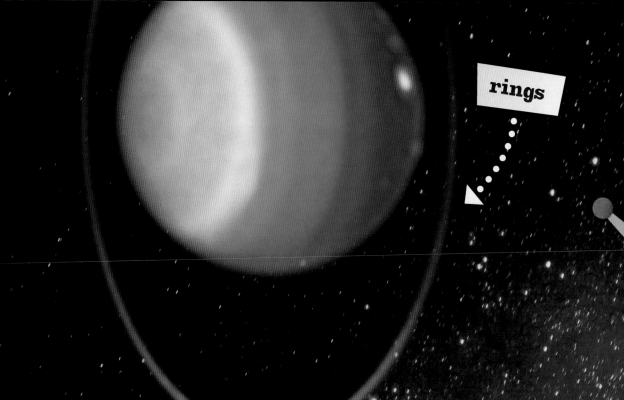

rings

Uranus

If you like summer, earthling, then Uranus is your planet. Summers here are 21 Earth-years long. And it's total daylight, all the time!

The trouble is, Uranus is so far from the sun that it's not exactly warm. This big ball of gas is *freezing*!

Let's spot some more moons.

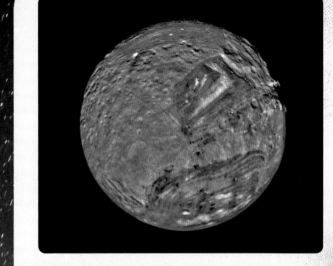

This is Miranda, one of
Uranus's 27 moons.

There's a moon!

And another!

melting ice	0°C
North Pole	- 40°C
Uranus	- 216°C

Aagghhh!

Neptune

Neptune's another giant gas ball. There's no ground to hit, so how about a skydive?

If you drop into those clouds, you'll hit winds faster than a fighter jet. You'll fall and fall, and then the crush of ice and gas will squash you flat! Ouch!

Fastest winds in the solar system

This is Triton, one of Neptune's 13 moons.

melting ice	0°C
North Pole	- 40°C
Neptune	- 214°C

Pluto and Beyond

Poor little rocky Pluto, way out on the edge of your solar system. You earthlings won't count it as a proper planet. You call it a **dwarf planet**.

Well, I like Pluto. It's so small there's hardly any **gravity** to hold anything on the ground – so it's perfect for giant leaps!

Time to get you home.

more dwarf planets

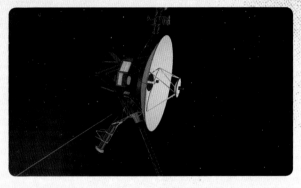

Voyager 1

This spacecraft has gone beyond Pluto and left our solar system. It has travelled further than anything else in human history.

melting ice	0°C
North Pole	– 40°C
Pluto	– 233°C

Earth

Call me an alien, but Earth really is way-out.

That comfy atmosphere full of air and cloud keeps it just right for you earthlings. Your heads won't boil and you can breathe.

And all that life! Crawly things, wiggly things – even vegetables! Freaky!

life

That's your planet, earthling.

Earth is awesome!

life

This is Earth's moon.

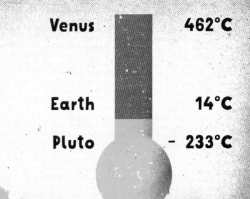

Venus   462°C

Earth   14°C

Pluto   - 233°C

Glossary

atmosphere: the layer of gas and cloud around a planet

°C: short for degrees Celsius, we use it to measure how hot or cold something is

days: days on Earth last 24 hours. That's how long it takes for the Earth to spin around once.

dwarf planet: a small planet

earthling: someone who lives on Earth

gas: something that isn't solid like rock, or liquid like water.

gravity: it pulls us down towards the ground so we stay on it

moon: a ball of rock or sometimes ice that circles a planet

planet: a big round ball of rock or gas that goes around a star

solar system: the group of planets that circles around a star, such as our sun

star: a big, very bright fiery ball, like our sun, but much, much further away

way-out: very unusual or crazy

Index

Bye!

Talk about it!

Which planet has two moons that are shaped like potatoes?

Which planet am I?

Read the clues to find out which planets are being described.

1. I have a moon called Triton.

2. I am the second biggest planet.

3. I have a Great Red Spot, which is a giant storm.

4. I am the smallest planet.

5. My atmosphere is so heavy it could squash you.

Answers: 1. Neptune; 2. Saturn; 3. Jupiter; 4. Mercury; 5. Venus

Pick Your Queen!

Compare the lives of two famous English queens – Elizabeth I and Queen Victoria. Who do you think is best?

Before reading

Talk about the queens – has your child ever heard of either of them? What do they think the queens will be like?

Look out for ...

... some long knickers! Which queen wore them?

... a red wig. Why did this queen wear wigs?

... a queen who kept wild animals as pets!

... a queen who wrote over 60 million words!

... a queen with her own private train.

PICK YOUR QUEEN!

CONTENTS

Rob Alcraft

Elizabeth I (Elizabeth the First) and Queen Victoria are two of the most famous queens from English history. You can pick the one you like best. But not yet! First, compare when they lived and how they lived – then you can decide.

Elizabeth I became queen in 1558. She died in 1603. We call this time in English history 'Elizabethan'.

45 years as queen

Queen Victoria became queen in 1837. She died in 1901. We call this time in English history 'Victorian'.

64 years
as queen

33

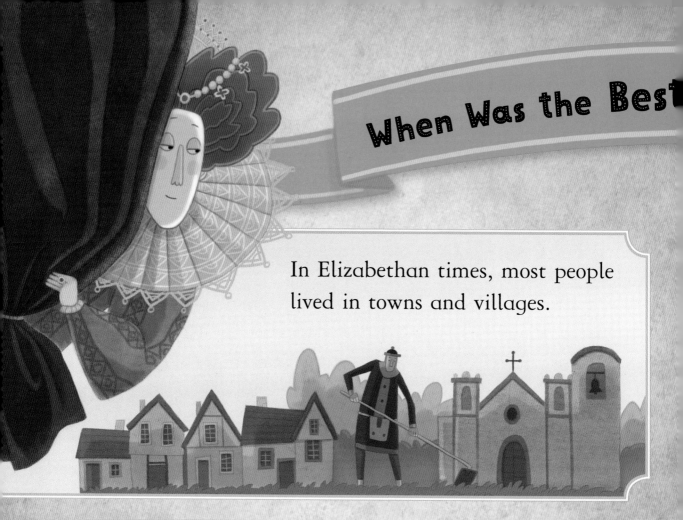

In Elizabethan times, most people lived in towns and villages.

Explorers were sailing around the world and travelling to new lands.

In London, there were new theatres. Plays were written by authors like William Shakespeare.

Time to Be Queen?

In Victorian times, most people lived in big smoky cities. There were new inventions like railways and electric lights.

Victoria was the queen of England, Scotland, Wales and Ireland. She was also the queen of other countries like Canada, India and Jamaica which were all part of the **British Empire**.

Elizabeth

Henry's other wives

Mum:
Anne Boleyn

was **executed** when Elizabeth was two years old

Dad:
Henry VIII

had six wives

Sister: Mary I

Brother:
Edward VI

Victoria

Dad: Prince Edward

died when Victoria was a baby

Mum:
Princess Victoria of
Saxe-Coburg-Saalfeld

Half-brother: Carl

Uncle:
King Leopold
of Belgium

Victoria's
favourite
uncle

Uncles: George IV
and William IV

Half-sister:
Feodora

37

Elizabeth lived in grand houses such as Hatfield House. She rode horses and went hunting.

Elizabeth learned languages like Latin and French. She was taught to make speeches. Her handwriting was excellent.

Victoria lived with her mum at Kensington Palace. She didn't have any friends.

Victoria had dolls and she made clothes for them.

Victoria learned languages and she was good at drawing and painting.

Elizabeth didn't get married. But lots of kings, princes and rich men asked if they could marry her. Elizabeth liked the attention and presents but she always said no!

Marry, or Not?

Victoria married her German cousin, Prince Albert, when she was 20. They had nine children. Can you see them all?

Elizabeth didn't just have pets, she had wild animals, too! She had **hawks**, dogs and horses for hunting. She even had bears for fighting!

Elizabeth's cuddliest pet was a small spaniel. She also had a monkey and a parrot.

Best Pets?

Victoria loved dogs. She had lots – Dash, Hector, Nero and many more! A small dog called Turi rode with Victoria in her carriage.

There was also Lory the parrot and Comus the horse.

Elizabeth owned hundreds of dresses and hundreds of jewels.

She wore **ruffs** and high heels.

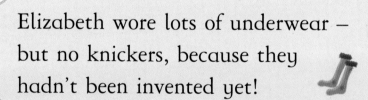

Elizabeth wore lots of underwear — but no knickers, because they hadn't been invented yet!

Elizabeth also wore red wigs because she was going bald.

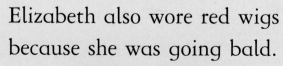

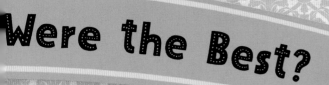

Were the Best?

When Victoria was young, she wore beautiful clothes.

Underneath, she wore long knickers and hoops to shape her dresses.

Sometimes, Victoria wore riding clothes.

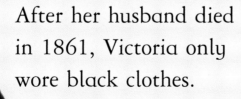

After her husband died in 1861, Victoria only wore black clothes.

Elizabeth enjoyed dancing, feasts and fireworks. She liked jelly, sugary **marzipan** and gingerbread.

Elizabeth enjoyed talking and playing card games.

Elizabeth loved books and music. She sang and played an instrument called a lute.

Victoria enjoyed picnics and drinking tea in her carriage.

She liked to eat cake and pie.

Victoria kept a diary and wrote letters to her children and friends. She probably wrote over 60 million words in her lifetime!

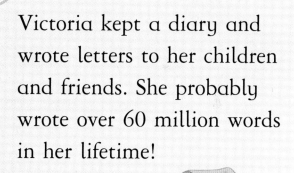

Whitehall Palace

Elizabeth owned many large palaces, like Whitehall Palace in London.

Nonsuch Palace

Elizabeth often moved between her palaces. Sometimes, up to 1000 people (friends, visitors and servants) moved with her!

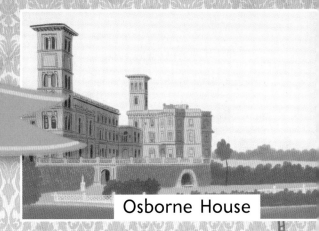

Osborne House

Victoria was the first ruling queen to live at Buckingham Palace.

Buckingham Palace

Victoria bought grand houses to stay in on holidays. She travelled on her own private train.

49

Elizabeth was the queen with the wigs! We call her time Elizabethan.

Elizabeth kept bears and had a monkey for a pet.

She liked to hunt, dance and eat gingerbread.

You choose!

Your Queen!

Victoria dressed in black and wore long knickers! We call her time Victorian.

Victoria had children, grandchildren and lots of dogs. She travelled by train and she loved tea and cake.

Which queen do you like best?

51

Royal Names

Edward VI: the sixth king called Edward (Edward the Sixth). It is written like this because lots of kings and queens have the same name. So we give them a Roman number, too.

Elizabeth I: the first queen called Elizabeth (Elizabeth the First)

George IV: the fourth king called George (George the Fourth)

Henry VIII: the eighth king called Henry (Henry the Eighth)

Mary I: the first queen called Mary (Mary the First)

William IV: the fourth king called William (William the Fourth)

Glossary

British Empire: a group of countries that were ruled by Britain

executed: put to death, killed

hawks: large birds, sometimes trained and used for hunting

marzipan: a sweet food made from sugar and almonds

ruffs: stiff frills worn round the neck

Index

Talk about it!

Would you rather live in my time, or in Queen Victoria's time? Why?

Royal match

Match the objects with the queen they belonged to.

Elizabeth I — Queen Victoria

Your Body, Inside Out

Find out how your body works, from the inside to the outside!

Before reading

Look at the contents list with your child. Can they work out which part of the body each section might be about?

Look out for ...

... a joint that can turn in a circle.

... a muscle that is hard to use.

... how many kilograms of food the average adult eats in a year.

... the number of times you blink every year.

... the number of different smells you can smell.

YOUR BODY, INSIDE OUT

CONTENTS

Vicky Shipton

START WITH YOUR SKELETON

Your skeleton is made up of bones. Without a skeleton, your body would be all floppy.

Babies are born with more than 300 bones, while adults have only 206. As babies grow, some of their bones join together.

biggest bone (femur)

smallest bone (stapes)

ball-and-socket joint

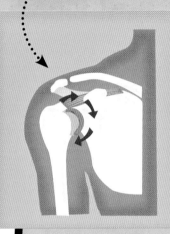

Joints are the parts of your skeleton where your bones meet up. Bones can't bend but joints can move in different ways.

Your shoulder joint can turn in a circle but your elbow joint can only bend.

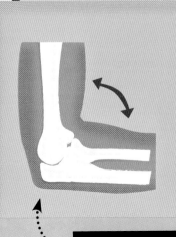

hinge joint

TRY THIS!

Can you lick your elbow? Almost *nobody* can!

MOVE YOUR MUSCLES

You need muscles to move your body –
around 600 of them! Muscles do lots of
jobs. You need them for any movement
you make, including walking, jumping,
dancing and even smiling.

Muscles are joined to your bones by
tough bands called tendons.

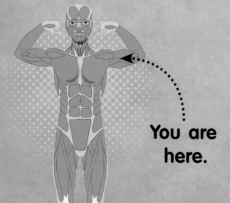

You are
here.

TRY THIS!
Some muscles are hard to use.
Try raising just one eyebrow!
Can you do it?

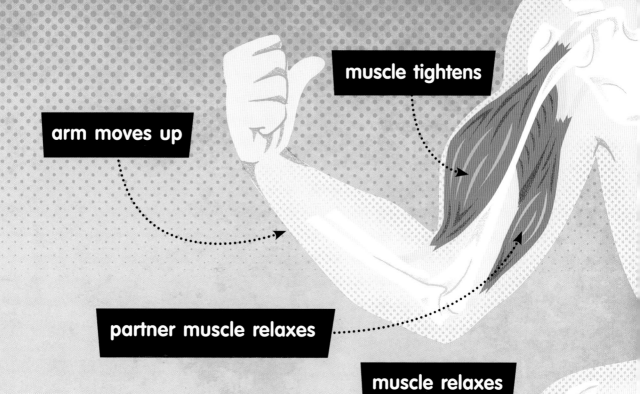

muscle tightens

arm moves up

partner muscle relaxes

muscle relaxes

Muscles work in pairs. When your upper-arm muscle tightens and pulls up your lower arm, its partner muscle relaxes. As your arm goes back down, the two muscles do the opposite jobs.

arm moves down

partner muscle tightens

PUMP YOUR
BLOOD

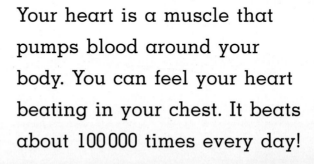

Blood brings **oxygen** and food to your muscles. It travels around your body in thin tubes called blood vessels. If you stretched out all these tubes, they'd go around the world more than twice!

You are here.

Your heart is a muscle that pumps blood around your body. You can feel your heart beating in your chest. It beats about 100 000 times every day!

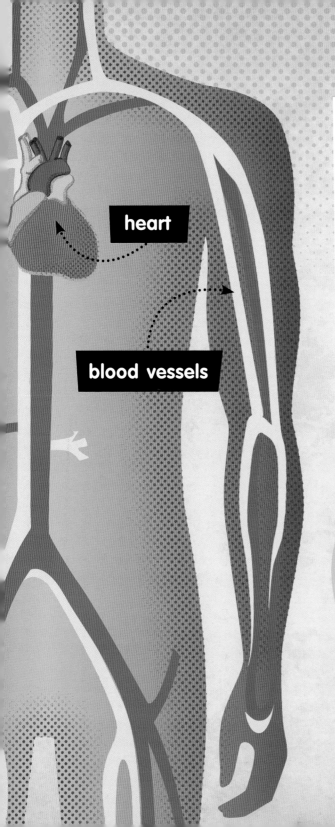

heart

blood vessels

A heart is shaped a bit like a fist but is often drawn differently.

TRY THIS!

Place your fingers gently on the inside of your wrist and feel your heartbeat. How many beats can you count in one minute?

BREATHE
IN AND OUT

Your body needs oxygen, which is in the air that we breathe. Oxygen helps your body turn food into energy. When you breathe in, your lungs fill up with air. Your lungs are like two sponges. They can hold about as much air as a football.

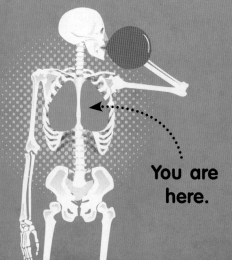

You are here.

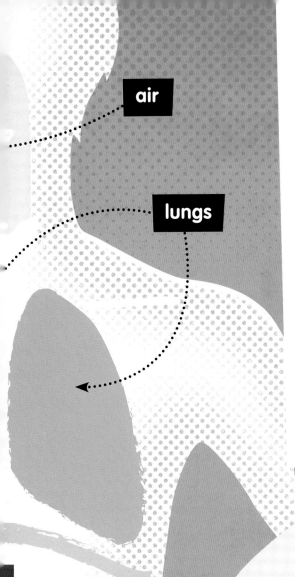

air

lungs

Your blood carries the air around your body, delivering oxygen. Then the unused air goes back to your lungs so you can breathe it out.

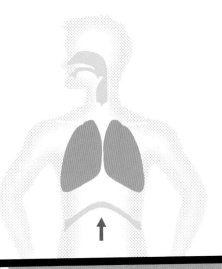

TRY THIS!

The more your muscles work, the more oxygen they need.

Sit down and count how many breaths you take in one minute. Then run on the spot for a minute and count your breaths again.

EAT UP!

Your body gets energy from food. Here's what happens when you eat an apple – or anything else! This whole process takes about a day.

1.

You chew the food and mix it with **saliva**.

You are here.

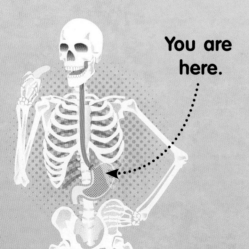

4.

The liquid travels into your **intestines**. Your body takes what it needs for energy.

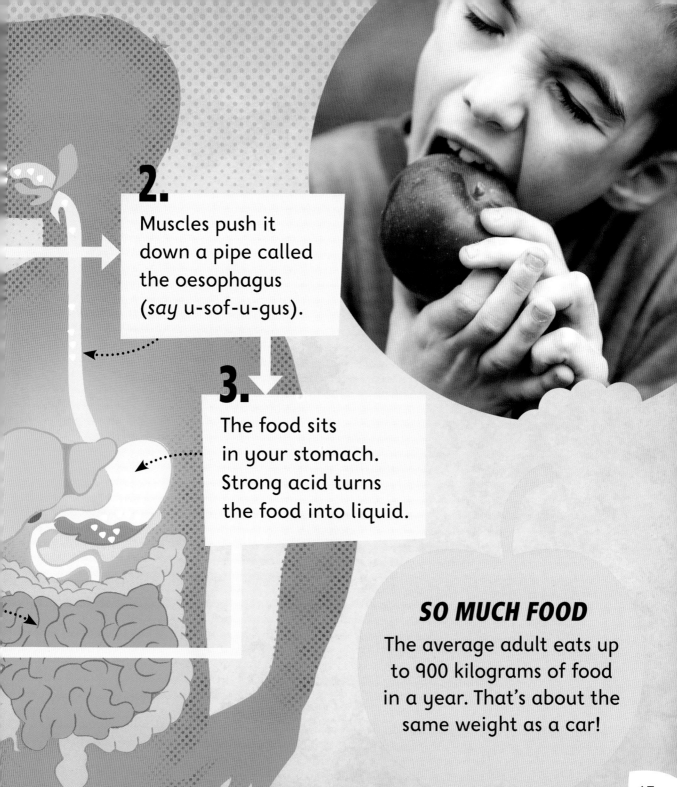

2.
Muscles push it down a pipe called the oesophagus (*say* u-sof-u-gus).

3.
The food sits in your stomach. Strong acid turns the food into liquid.

SO MUCH FOOD

The average adult eats up to 900 kilograms of food in a year. That's about the same weight as a car!

CONTROL CENTRE

Your brain controls your whole body. It sends **signals** to different parts of your body to make them move. These signals travel around your body through the **nervous system**.

You are here.

brain

Your brain even controls things you don't think about, like breathing and pumping blood.

nerves

Your brain controls memory and feelings, too.

This part controls memory.

This part controls feelings.

TRY THIS!

Pat your head with one hand and rub your tummy in a circle with the other. Can your brain send the right signals to the right body parts?

SEEING AND HEARING

You see things when light bounces off them and into your eyes. Signals are sent from the back of your eyes to your brain.

You are here.

pupil

nerve

eyeball

You blink so your eyes don't get dry. Some people blink up to 50 times per minute. This adds up to more than 26 million blinks every year!

You hear things when sound waves travel through the air. These sound waves enter your ears and send signals to your brain.

ear drum

nerve

TRY THIS!

Your ears help you balance. Try spinning around and then standing still. Are you dizzy and wobbly? That's because fluid in your ear keeps spinning after you have stopped. Your brain is getting mixed-up signals!

SMELLING AND TASTING

You can smell around 10000 different smells – both good and bad ones!

Smells travel into your nose through your nostrils. Then the nerve cells behind your nose send messages to your brain to tell you what the smell is.

You are here.

nostrils

nerve cells

You taste food with your tongue. It helps you know if something tastes sweet, salty, sour or bitter.

Your sense of smell and taste work together. If something smells bad, it usually tastes bad, too!

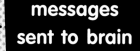

messages sent to brain

TRY THIS!

You need saliva to taste. Try drying your tongue with a tissue before you eat something. Can you still taste it?

WRAPPING IT UP

If you could lay your skin flat, it would cover your bed. But don't – it's keeping your insides in! Skin also keeps your body safe from **infection**.

You are here.

You grow new skin and lose old skin all the time. Every single minute, up to 50000 tiny flakes of dead skin can fall off you!

hair

skin

close-up of skin flakes

BRRR!

When you are cold or scared, muscles in your skin tighten and make small bumps called goose bumps. These make the hairs on your skin stand on end.

YOUR HAIR

You have hair all over your body. The only parts of your body with no hair are the soles of your feet and the palms of your hands.

You are here.

close-up of a hair

NO PAIN

Hair is made of dead cells. That's why it doesn't hurt when you get your hair cut!

Your body and all its different parts are **amazing** – from the inside out!

GLOSSARY

infection: a disease or illness that enters the body

intestines: long tubes under your stomach that food passes through

nervous system: nerves all over your body that move signals to and from your brain

oxygen: a part of air that your body needs for energy

saliva: liquid in your mouth that helps you chew and taste food

signals: messages that are sent around your body

INDEX

Talk about it!

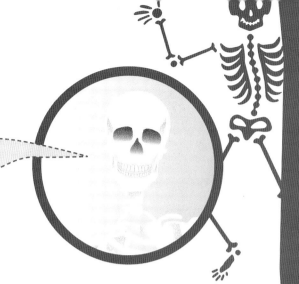

What is the most interesting fact you found out from reading this text?

True or false?

Decide whether these statements about the human body are true or false.

1. The smallest bone in your body is inside your ear.

2. Most people can easily lick their elbow.

3. The harder your body works, the less you need to breathe.

4. Your heart pumps your blood all round your body.

5. You blink so that your eyes don't get dry.

6. The food eaten by an average adult every year weighs about the same as a blue whale.

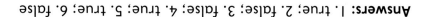

Answers: 1. true; 2. false; 3. false; 4. true; 5. true; 6. false

Flight or Fright?

Learn about the history of flying machines.

Before reading

Talk about the title of the book. What might be frightening about flying? How many different types of flying machine can your child think of?

Look out for ...

... some animals that tested a hot-air balloon.

... a flying machine made from cows' intestines!

... the *Mosquito*. It was held together by screws and glue, but the glue came unstuck!

... a plane that flew for less than a minute.

... a plane designed to take tourists into space.

FLIGHT OR FRIGHT?

CONTENTS

Janine Scott

Fly Like Birds

Long ago, people wanted to fly. They climbed up high, put on wings and flapped – and then they jumped! They usually landed in a heap.

Since then, people have made many different flying machines. It took lots of **trial and error** before humans built a machine that could fly.

Testing the machines was often **trial** *and* TERROR!

The birdman flying machine was one
of the earliest flying machines.

Fear in the Air

In 1783, French brothers Joseph and Jacques Montgolfier designed a large hot-air balloon. They built a fire on the ground and held the opening of the balloon over the fire.

The balloon went up but the smell was terrible – they had put old shoes and rotten meat on the fire!

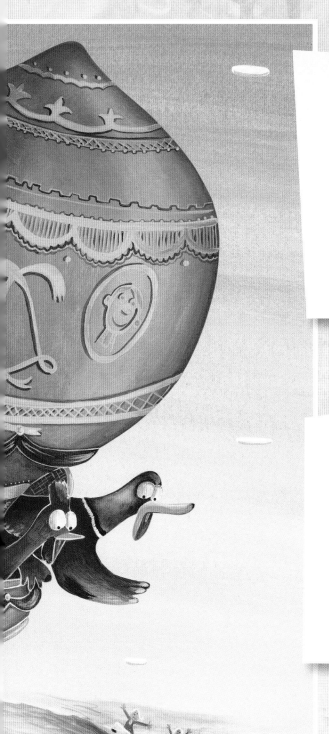

The Montgolfier brothers got their balloon idea when they saw paper scraps floating near a fire. To test their idea, they filled paper bags with smoke.

Trial and TERROR!

The brothers were afraid to test the balloon themselves, so they sent a sheep, a duck and a rooster up instead! Luckily, the animals landed safely.

Glider Rider

A glider is a flying machine that has no engine. Its specially shaped wings help it glide through the air.

Otto Lilienthal was a German glider inventor known as the 'Glider King'. In 1894, Otto built a big hill, which he used to **launch** his gliders.

Otto Lilienthal flew his first glider in 1891.

Trial and error

Otto made at least nine different gliders. Over five years, he went for more than 2000 glider flights.

Trial and TERROR!

On 9th August 1896, Otto crashed his glider. Sadly, he died from his injuries the next day.

Otto Lilienthal

Fiery Flight

Airships are big balloons with bags of gas inside them. This gas is lighter than air, so it helps the airship rise. The first airships were filled with **flammable** gas.

Trial and error

In early airships that were trialled, the bags that held the gas were made from cows' **intestines**. The intestines of 250 000 cows were needed for one airship!

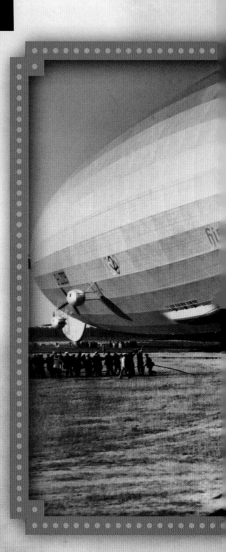

The *Hindenburg* was a huge airship.
It had a dining room and a lounge.

The *Hindenburg* exploded
in 1937. Sadly, many
people on board died.

The *Hindenburg*'s first
flight was in 1936.

87

Sky Flyer

On 14th December 1903, the first **powered** aeroplane took flight – and then crashed! The *Flyer*, which was built by the Wright brothers, flew for just 3.5 seconds.

Three days later, the *Flyer* flew again – this time for 12 seconds, at Kitty Hawk in the United States of America (USA). Kitty Hawk was a good place for flying. It had strong winds, which helped the *Flyer* take off, and soft sand for crash landings!

Trial and error

The Wright brothers built a **wind tunnel**. They used it to test about 200 different wing shapes.

The *Flyer* took its first proper flight on 17th December 1903.

Trial and TERROR!

The Wright brothers flew the *Flyer* three more times after the first flight. After its fourth flight, a big wind flipped the *Flyer*, damaging it. It never flew again.

Wooden Wonder

Most aeroplanes today are made of metal. However, the *Mosquito* was made of wood. It was designed in England and flown during the Second World War. It was one of the fastest aeroplanes flown in the war.

The plane was held together with screws and glue. When the *Mosquito* flew in hot places, the glue sometimes came unstuck!

Flying fact

In England during the Second World War, furniture makers and piano makers helped make the planes!

The *Mosquito* was first flown in 1940.

Trial and TERROR!

One of the *Mosquito*'s nicknames was the '**Timber** Terror'.

Floating Flyer

A flying boat is a plane that can land on water. The biggest flying boat ever built was the *Spruce Goose*. It was made out of wood. Most people thought it was too big to fly.

Trial and TERROR!

The *Spruce Goose* was designed to carry 750 soldiers during the Second World War. Unfortunately, it wasn't ready in time!

Trial and error

The *Spruce Goose* was tested only once. It flew for less than one minute! It was never used again.

The *Spruce Goose* took its first and only flight on 2nd November 1947.

In a Spin

Helicopters fly up, down, backwards, forwards and sideways. They can even **hover** in one place.

Helicopters have two **rotors** that spin around – a main rotor and a tail rotor. Without a tail rotor, a helicopter would turn in circles!

Igor Sikorsky made the first successful American helicopter in 1939.

tail rotor

Trial and TERROR!

Igor's first helicopter went backwards and sideways. However, it had trouble going forwards!

Trial and error

Igor made so many changes to his helicopter design, it was nicknamed 'Igor's Nightmare'!

main rotor

Igor Sikorsky first flew his helicopter on 14th September 1939.

Invisible!

The B-2 stealth bomber is a warplane. It was designed in secret and first flown in 1989. It has a smooth shape and special paint that make it almost impossible for **radars** to find.

Flying fact

Sometimes B-2s drop dummy bombs. These look like bombs but they do not explode. They are used during training exercises.

The B-2 stealth bomber is painted grey, which makes it hard to see in the sky.

Trial and TERROR!

Some B-2 flights are 40 hours long. There is a toilet in the plane but there are no walls around it!

Space Plane

SpaceShipTwo is a plane designed to take tourists into space. It went on its first powered test flight in April 2013.

A plane called *WhiteKnightTwo* carries *SpaceShipTwo* into the sky and lets it go in mid-air. *SpaceShipTwo* then flies into space.

A flight will last about 2.5 hours, but the tourists will be in space for only a few minutes. In space, there is no **gravity** to pull things towards the ground. So the people can float around inside the plane!

Trial and error

SpaceShipTwo's first test flight was not in space. It was over a desert.

SpaceShipTwo

WhiteKnightTwo

Trial and TERROR!

SpaceShipTwo can re-enter Earth's **atmosphere** at any angle – even upside down!

Glossary

atmosphere: the layer of gas and cloud around Earth

flammable: likely to catch fire easily and burn quickly

gravity: it pulls us down towards the ground so we stay on it

hover: to stay in one place in the air

intestines: long tubes under the stomach that food passes through

launch: to start something moving

powered: moved with the help of an engine

radars: machines that use radio waves to find objects

rotors: the spinning parts of a helicopter; the main rotor helps the helicopter to lift off the ground

timber: wood

trial and error: to keep trying and learning from your mistakes, until you are successful

wind tunnel: a huge tube with air moving inside it

Index

Talk about it!

Which of the flying machines would you most like to fly in? Why?

Word search

Can you find all these different flying machines in the grid?

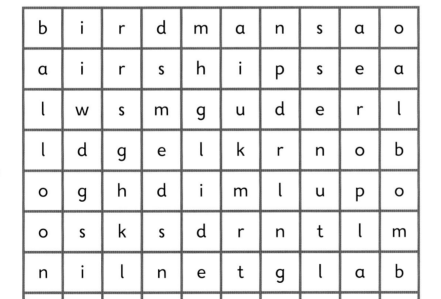

b	i	r	d	m	a	n	s	a	o
a	i	r	s	h	i	p	s	e	a
l	w	s	m	g	u	d	e	r	l
l	d	g	e	l	k	r	n	o	b
o	g	h	d	i	m	l	u	p	o
o	s	k	s	d	r	n	t	l	m
n	i	l	n	e	t	g	l	a	b
s	r	t	r	r	c	n	i	n	e
h	e	l	i	c	o	p	t	e	r

birdman

balloon

glider

airship

aeroplane

helicopter

bomber

Spread the Word

Find out about three famous people who changed the way we communicate: William Caxton, Alexander Graham Bell and Tim Berners-Lee.

Before reading

Talk about the three people in this text. Has your child ever heard of them? Flip through the text to get a sense of who they are and what they did.

Look out for ...

... one of the first books printed in England.

... the smallest book in the world. Its pages are only a millimetre big!

... Alexander Bell's first invention.

... things Alexander Bell invented.

... which year the first ever website went online.

SPREAD THE WORD

CONTENTS

Ciaran Murtagh

Introduction

People **communicate** all the time. Especially me! I'm always trying to spread the word. Sometimes I tap words into an email or a text. Sometimes I talk to people face-to-face. Sometimes I speak to people using a phone. And sometimes I spread the word through a book – like this!

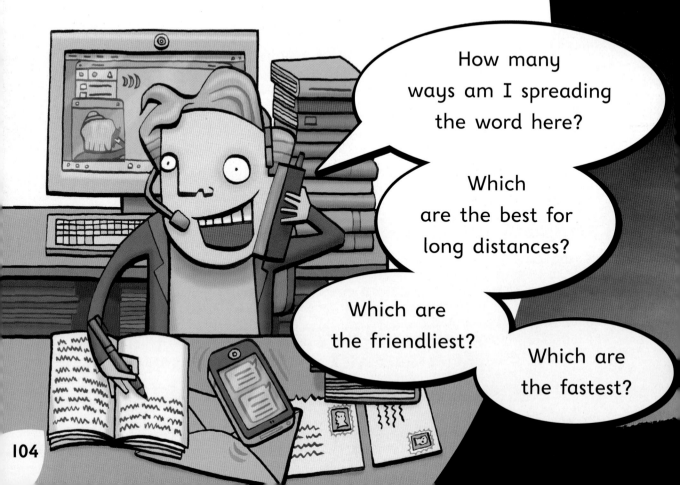

How many ways am I spreading the word here?

Which are the best for long distances?

Which are the friendliest?

Which are the fastest?

But I wouldn't be able to do half of these things if it hadn't been for:

William Caxton,

Alexander Graham Bell

and **Tim Berners-Lee**.

They found ways to help spread the word all around the world.

William Caxton

[What: **The printing press**
When: **The 1400s**]

Nobody knows exactly when William Caxton was born.

It could have been 1419. Or maybe 1420 ... ?

It was about 1421.

He grew up in Kent, England, then went to London to train to be a **merchant**.

Caxton sold British wool and bought **goods** from other European countries. On his travels, Caxton saw a printing press printing a book.

Without a printing press, if you wanted a book, you had to pay someone to write it out for you. This took a long time and cost lots of money.

With the printing press, it got quicker and cheaper to make books.

I'd like a book, please.

Come back in a year!

Caxton realised what an important invention the printing press was and he learned how to use it. ★

An early printing press

1. The printer put letters on a board to spell out words.

Messy business!

2. He covered the letters in ink and pulled down on a handle.

Beard at risk!

3. The inky letters were pressed onto a piece of paper and a page in a book was made.

Ta-da!

In 1476, Caxton set up a printing press in London. One of the first books printed in England was *The Canterbury Tales* by Geoffrey Chaucer. It was so popular that another version was printed with pictures!

Thanks to Caxton's printing press, more people could afford to buy books – although they were still quite expensive. And there wasn't much choice at first!

Got anything else?

Caxton printed about 100 different books. Now millions of books are printed all around the world every year. Printing presses are faster and books are cheaper.

BONKERS BOOK FACT

The world's smallest book is *Shiki no Kusabana*. It's a Japanese book of flowers with pages less than 1mm big!

In fact, without printing presses, you wouldn't be holding this book in your hand right now!

Alexander Graham Bell

What: The telephone

When: The late 1800s

Alexander Graham Bell was born in Edinburgh, Scotland, in 1847. He began inventing when he was just a boy.

12-year-old Bell and his first invention – a de-husking machine

Boy, you're a genius!

The wheat goes in here with the husk still on the grain. Then it comes out with the husk taken off!

Bell

A school for the deaf in Boston, United States of America (USA)

When Bell grew up, he gave lessons to deaf people to help them communicate better. He worked in Canada and the USA. It was in the USA that Bell invented the telephone.

Bell wanted to find a way to talk to people who were a long way away. He invented something that would allow his voice to travel great distances.

On 10th March 1876, Bell used a telephone wire to send a message to his assistant in the next room. He said, "Mr Watson, come here. I want to see you!"

You could have just come and talked to me!

It was the first phone call! However, there was still a lot of work to do before Bell had made an actual telephone.

Bell's first telephone

Telephones helped people to communicate with each other more quickly and easily than ever before.

Over the years, telephones got better and better, and worked over longer and longer distances.

1890

1929

1954

Bell's other great inventions:

One of the first metal detectors

A record-breaking hydrofoil boat

A tool to find icebergs

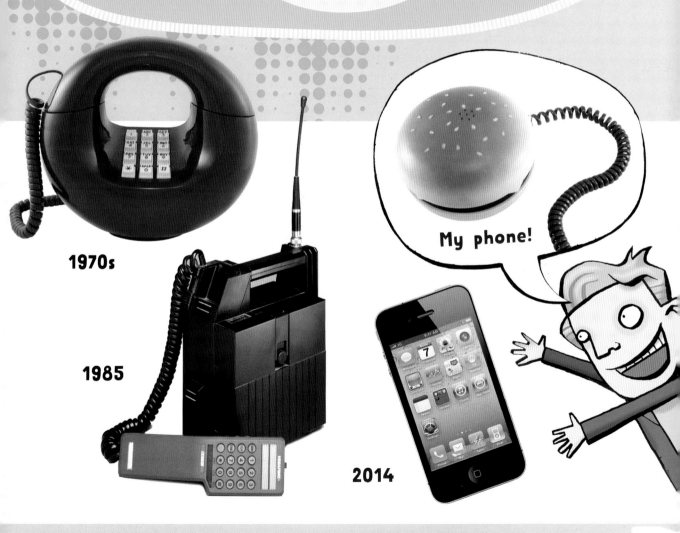

My phone!

1970s

1985

2014

Tim Berners-Lee

What: The World Wide Web

When: The early 1990s

Tim Berners-Lee was born in London, UK, in 1955. When he was a child, he was a keen **train-spotter**. He learned about **electronics** by playing with his model train set.

Berners-Lee went to study at Oxford University.

He became very interested in computers. He even built a computer out of an old television and a **processor**.

Hey! We were watching that!

Berners-Lee wanted to find a way of using computers to communicate with people all over the world quickly and for free. This is how he came up with the **World Wide Web**.

The World Wide Web is a way for people to use the **Internet** to communicate with each other. Lots of information is joined together in a 'web' and is shared on their computers.

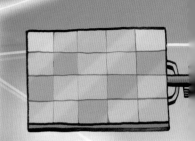

To thank Berners-Lee for his ideas and hard work, Queen Elizabeth II made him a **knight** in 2004.

One's web address is www.royal.gov.uk

Today, Berners-Lee works with people from around the world to improve the World Wide Web.

Glossary

communicate: to share information

electronics: the science of electricity

goods: items that can be bought or sold

husk: the shell around a grain of wheat

hydrofoil: a boat with wings that lift the boat out of the water

Internet: network of computers

knight: someone who is given a special honour by a king or queen

merchant: a person who sells things to another person

metal detectors: machines that help people to find metal objects

processor: a machine that handles information

train-spotter: a person who spots trains for a hobby

World Wide Web: part of the Internet designed to help users find their way around it

Index

Talk about it!

Which inventor do you think made the biggest difference to how we communicate? Why?

Who am I?

Match the facts with the inventors.

I trained as a merchant, and got my big idea when I was abroad on business.

I made my first invention when I was 12.

I learned about electronics by playing with trains.

OXFORD
UNIVERSITY PRESS

Great Clarendon Street, Oxford, OX2 6DP, United Kingdom

Oxford University Press is a department of the University of Oxford. It furthers the University's objective of excellence in research, scholarship, and education by publishing worldwide. Oxford is a registered trade mark of Oxford University Press in the UK and in certain other countries

Way-out Day Out text © Rob Alcraft 2014
Illustrations by Philip Giordano

Pick Your Queen! text © Rob Alcraft 2014
Illustrations by Shahab Shamshirsaz

Your Body, Inside Out text © Vicky Shipton 2014
Illustrations by Chantel de Sousa

Flight or Fright? text © Janine Scott 2014
Illustrations by Oliver Daumas

Spread the Word text © Ciaran Murtagh 2014
Illustrations by Glen McBeth

The moral rights of the authors have been asserted

This Edition published in 2019

British Library Cataloguing in Publication Data
Data available

ISBN: 978-0-19-276971-8

10 9 8 7 6 5 4 3 2 1

Paper used in the production of this book is a natural, recyclable product made from wood grown in sustainable forests. The manufacturing process conforms to the environmental regulations of the country of origin.

Printed in China

Acknowledgements
Series Editor: Nikki Gamble

Way-out Day Out

The publisher would like to thank the following for permission to reproduce photographs: **p9:** OUP/Corbis; **p14** and **p15:** Shutterstock; **p19:** Shutterstock; **p22:** Tristan3D/Alamy; **p24** and **p25:** Vadim Sadovski/Shutterstock; **p24:** CVADRAT/Shutterstock.

All other images provided by NASA and Oxford University Press

Pick Your Queen!

The publisher would like to thank the following for permission to reproduce photographs: **p32:** National Portrait Gallery, London; **p33:** National Portrait Gallery, London

Your Body, Inside Out

Designed and typeset by Cristina Neri, Canary Graphic Design

The publisher would like to thank the following for permission to reproduce photographs: **p60:** YanLev/Shutterstock; **p65:** Cara Slifka/Stocksy; **p69:** UpperCut Images/Alamy; **p71:** George Doyle/Onyx/F1online; **p73:** Science Photo Library; **p75:** Steve Gschmeissner/Science Photo Library; Ron Nickel/Design Pics/Corbis

Flight or Fright?

Designed and typeset by Fiona Lee, Pounce Creative

The publisher would like to thank the following for permission to reproduce photographs: **p80** and **p81:** Bettmann/Corbis; **p84** and **p85:** Bettmann/Corbis; **p85:** DIZ Muenchen GmbH, Sueddeutsche Zeitung Photo/Alamy; **p86** and **p87:** Corbis; **p87:** Bettmann/Corbis; **p89:** RGB Ventures LLC dba SuperStock/Alamy; **p90** and **p91:** Popperfoto/Getty Images; **p92** and **p93:** Time & Life Pictures/Getty Images; **p94** and **p95:** Popperfoto/Getty Images; **p95:** PF-(sdasm1)/Alamy; **p96** and **p97:** CNP/Sygma/Corbis; **p98** and **p99:** REX

Spread the Word

The publisher would like to thank the following for permission to reproduce photographs: **p105:** Fotolibra; Alamy/Pictorial press Ltd; Getty Images/Hank Morgan/Science Faction; **p106:** Fotolibra; Mary Evans picture Library; **p109:** Alamy/NTPL/Mark Fiennes; **p111:** Quang Ho/Shutterstock; **p112:** Alamy/Pictorial press Ltd; Getty Images; **p113:** Getty Images/Time Life Pictures; **p115:** Alamy/Picture Library; **p116:** Science Museum/Science and Society Picture Library; Science Museum/Science and Society Picture Library; Mary Evans picture Library; **p117:** Basement Stock/Alamy; Science Museum/Science and Society Picture Library; lamy/Pumpkin Pie; Shutterstock/Christopher Dodge; **p118:** Getty Images/Hank Morgan/Science Faction; **Background images:** Thaiview/Shutterstock; Semisatch/Shutterstock; saicle/Shutterstock; arigato/Shutterstock; skyboysv/Shutterstock

All other images Shutterstock

Cover images Shutterstock